Finding Q: The Great Alphabet Hunt

Paula Curtis Taylorson

illustrated by Hussain Anwar

Finding Q : The Great Alphabet Hunt

This is a work of fiction.

Text and Illustrations copyrighted

by Paula Curtis Taylorson ©2021

Library of Congress Control Number: 2021904828

All rights reserved. No part of this book may be

reproduced, transmitted, or stored in an information retrieval

system in any form or by any means,

graphic, electronic, or mechanical without prior written

permission from the author.

Printed in the United States of America

A 2 Z Press LLC

PO Box 582

Deleon Springs, FL 32130

bestlittleonlinebookstore.com

sizemore3630@aol.com

440-241-3126

ISBN: 978-1-954191-18-1

Dedication

Thank you to those who read to me and those who listened to me read.

Quintessa is a **quizzical queen.**

She has some **queer** and **quaint** ideas in her head.

Looking for **Q** words is **quite** a tall order. Yet her **quest** is to find more words than she's ever read!

The **quotable** King **Qwayden**
is here to **quietly** assist

and **quicken** the pace of the search.

Prince **Quacky** the duck **questions** his King,

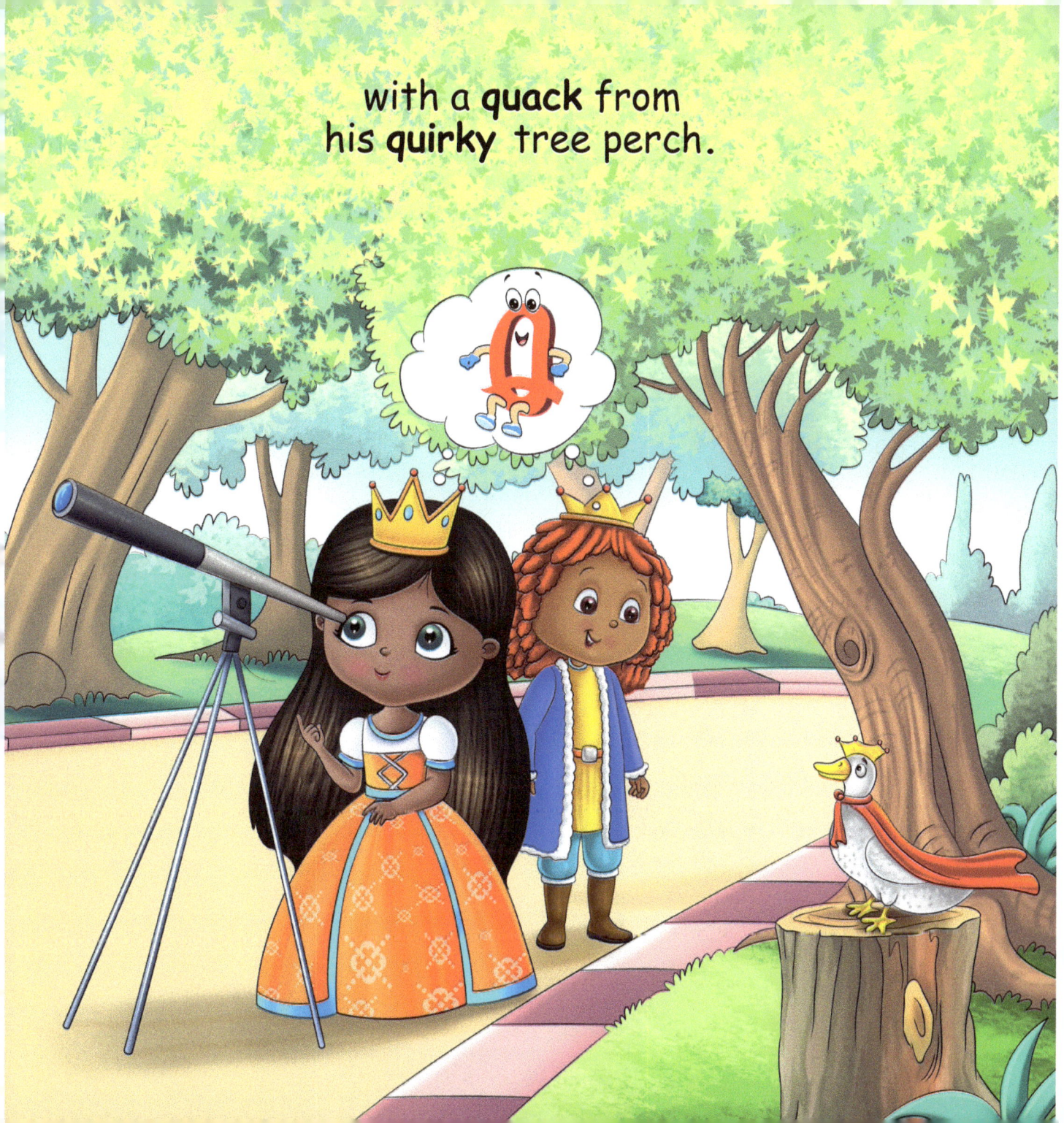
with a **quack** from his **quirky** tree perch.

A **quarterback** from **Quebec** is feeling **queasy** but hungry,

so he tucks into some **quiche** made with **quark**.

and they **quickstep** their way to the park.

Quasimodo's in a bit of a **quandary**. He's stepped into a **quagmire** filled with **quicksand**.

Luckily, he's saved by a large **quantity** of rope thrown to him by an Australian **quokka** from **Queensland**!

The King and Queen find a couple of **quails** having a **quibble**.

Neither one of them is willing to **quit**.

While a **Quartermaster** from a ship called the HMS **Quasar**

says, 'They should **quieten** their **quarrel** a bit!'

A beautiful **Quora** sits in a **Quercus** tree.

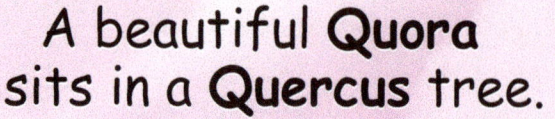

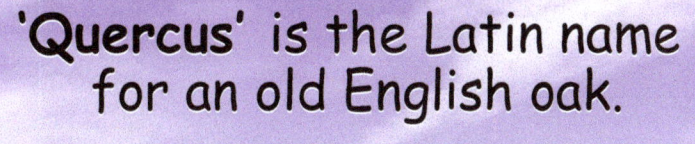
'Quercus' is the Latin name for an old English oak.

There is a set of **quintuplets** looking up from below and

They **quiver** and **quaver** with joy.

They are **quenching** their thirst with a **quart** of fresh milk

that was delivered by **Quentin**, the grocery store boy!

Quintessa queenly sits at her desk. With her **quill** pen she writes a **quick** love letter

to a **quarryman** mining rock crystal quartz, making **quintessentially** sure that he doesn't forget her!

to make a **quilt** for **Qwaydon's** birthday surprise!

They'll play **quoits** in the garden
and **quidditch** on brooms,
and feast on **quinoa** (keen waa),
quesadillas, and fries.

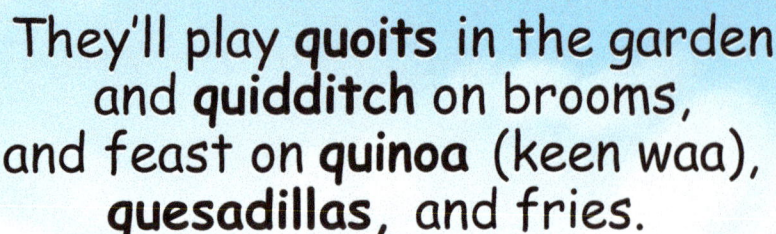

The **Q**'s have been found and **Quintessa** is resting,
She is satisfied there are no more in the **queue**.

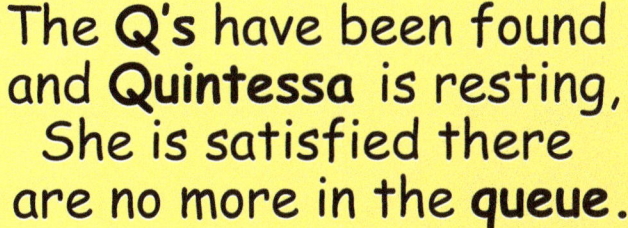

The **Q** had its turn in this alphabet hunt and there is always more **quizzing** to do!

The End

My Very Own 'Q' Words:

_____

_____

_____

_____

_____

_____

_____

_____

_____

_____

_____

Glossary

Page 1. **Quintessa** : a girl or woman's name
Quizzical : odd, comical, puzzling
Queen : a female leader, a wife of a king

Page 2. **Queer** : odd, strange, not the usual
Quaint: charming, pleasant and old-fashioned, cute

Page 3. **Q** : a letter
Quite : really, truly
Quest : a search, to find something

Page 4. **Quotable** : to repeat what is said
Qwayden : a boy or man's name
Quietly : without making much noise

Page 5. **Quicken** : move in a fast way

Page 6. Prince **Quacky** : the duck in this book
Questions : something asked to gain information or investigate something

Page 7. **Quack** : the noise a duck makes
Quirky : odd, something peculiar to one or something that no one else has or does, an action or behaviour, a quick movement

Page 8. **Quarterback** : a football player who throws the ball
Quebec's : a country
Queasy : an upset tummy, uneasy feeling

Page 9. **Quiche** : food like a pie with eggs and cheese and other ingredients
Quark : a soft white spreadable cheese

Page 10. **Qadisha** : a girl or woman's name
Qatar : a country off the Persian Gulf under British protection

Page 11. **Quickstep** : walk fast

Page 12. **Quasimodo**'s : a made-up character in the story "The Hunchback of Note Dame"
Quandary : a dilemma or sticky situation, not sure what to do
Quagmire : a bog or a marsh area
Quicksand : an area of soft ground that a person can sink into

Page 13. **Quantity** : the amount or number of something
Australian **quokka** : is a cute, small, short-tailed member of the kangaroo family.
Queensland : an area in Australia – a country

Page 14. **Quails** : small birds
Quibble : to argue

Page 15. **Quit** : stop doing something

Page 16. **Quartermaster** : an officer on a boat or ship
HMS **Quasar** : a famous and large ship

Page 17. **Quieten** : to decrease noise or activity
Quarrel : arguing, disagreeing

Page 18. **Quora** : a bird
Quercus tree : a large oak tree

Page 20. **Quintuplets** : a group of five

Page 21. **Quetzal** bird : a bird

Page 22. **Quillfish** : a long fish that looks like an eel
Quince : a small tree bearing fruit

Page 23. **Quiver** : shake, shiver softly
Quaver : shake, shiver more so than quiver

Page 24. **Quenching** : to satisfy
Quart : a measure $\frac{1}{4}$ of a gallon

Page 25. **Quentin** : a boy or man's name

Page 26. **Queenly** : in the fashion or manner of a queen
Quill : the part of a long feather
Quick : fast

Page 27. **Quarryman** : workers in a quarry, a pit to get stone from
Quartz : a stone with value as a gem
Quintessentially : something that is really perfect

Page 28. **Qualified** : some able to do a task
Quilter : one who sews quilts

Page 29. **Quilt** : a large hand-sewn quilt from pieces of fabric

Page 30. **Quoits** : a game with objects are thrown around a stake
Quidditch : an imaginary game where players fly on broomsticks
Quinoa (keen-waa) : a super food filled with protein and vitamins
Quesadillas : food

Page 31. **Queue** : a file or line of waiting people or tasks

Page 32. **Quizzing** : asking to obtain information or answers

Paula Curtis-Taylorson Lives in Marston Mortaine England. She is a full-time secondary school teacher of English and English Literature. She was amongst the first of the initial students to graduate from the Uk's first BA (Hons) Creative Writing Program at the University of Bedfordshire.

Her first love is poetry and rhyme and she works hard to inspire and teach appreciation of the subject to all age groups. Many of her students have gone on to be successful writers.

A2Z Press LLC

A2Z Press LLC published this work. A2Z Press LLC is a publishing company created by Terrie Sizemore for the purpose of publishing literary works by new and aspiring writers. All content is G-rated. We welcome your submissions of ideas for children's literature as well as adult and self-help topics. Science and medicine, holidays and other interesting topics are all welcome. Submit queries to sizemore3630@aol.com or PO Box 582 Deleon Springs, FL 32130

www.ingramcontent.com/pod-product-compliance
Lightning Source LLC
Chambersburg PA
CBHW061105070526
44579CB00011B/140